The Ultimate Crocheting Guide for Beginners!

The Easiest Step by Step Guide with Illustrations and Pictures

Table of Contents

Introduction

I want to thank you and congratulate you for purchasing this book:

"Crochet: The Ultimate Crocheting Guide for Beginners!"

This book contains proven steps and strategies regarding everything that you need to know on how to begin crocheting. This book will teach you the basic stitches that you need to know first including the proper way to wind the yarn to your fingers and the way you should hold your hook. You will also learn the different hook sizes and the thickness of yarn that suits each hook size.

This book includes simple patterns to get you started. Hopefully, by the time that you have finished reading this book, you will be able to create your own crocheted masterpiece.

Thanks again for purchasing this book, I hope you enjoy it!

CHAPTER 1

Start with the Basics

At first glance, crocheting seems to have its own language. When you read a crochet pattern, you will get lost in translation if you don't know the different terminologies and abbreviations used. The terms are usually abbreviated to create ease in reading and writing. As you learn (and as you hone your craft), you will see that it is much easier to follow the abbreviated instructions, and you can almost see the finished project even if you don't see the picture.

It is important to know and memorize the different crochet stitches as well as their abbreviations and symbols. Most patterns use abbreviations in their instructions, and there are patterns that use diagrams where the symbols are illustrated for the different rounds.

Learning the Language of Crochet

Of course, it would be easier for you to understand how to crochet if you know how to read and understand the abbreviations you'd often see in those crochet patterns.

Listed below are the said types of stitches, their abbreviations, symbols, and what they mean.

Alt

Alt means Alternate, and is symbolized by the given image. This simply means that you have to work rows on every other stitch or row.

Approx

This stands for Approximate. It's not really a "stitch" per se, but it means that you have to work stitches close or approximate to some of the stitches you already have.

Beg

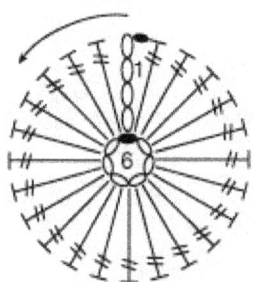

Beg stands for beginning, which means that it is where you have to start working on your stitches. The symbol varies depending on the kind of project you're doing.

For example, you're doing project that you have to crochet in a circular motion. The middle point is labeled 6, and the beginning point is labeled 1. Check out the sample below.

Bet

Bet stands for between, which means you have to work a stitch between two points.

BL (Bl)

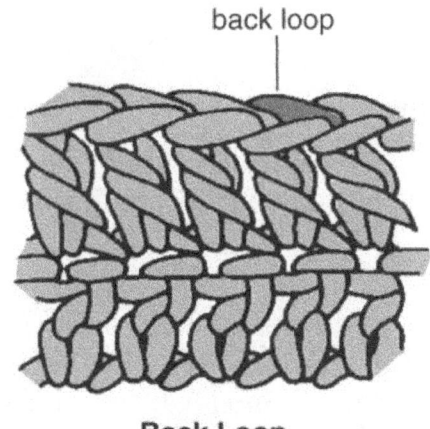

back loop

Back Loop

Short for Back Loop, this means that you have to insert your hook under the back loop and then continue making the stitch you see on your pattern.

BP

BP stands for Back Post. These are the stitches that appear on the receding side of the fabric.

BPDC

$$\text{☂} = \text{BP dc}$$

Meanwhile, BPDC stands for Back Post Double Crochet. These are stitches that start being made from normal double crochet position, and then followed by creating a normal row.

BPSC

BPSC means Back Post Single Crochet. These stitches are done by inserting hook from back to front around the stitch that was designated, and then use two loops for yarning over.

BPTC

Now, this one is about Back Post Triple Crochet, or the act of creating receding triple crochet stitches, mostly by yarning over the hook all the way to the front.

CC

Cc stands for contrast color. This means you have to use contrasting yarn colors for the project you're working on.

Ch

Ch stands for Chain, which means you have to create chain stitches. You can do this by making a set of looping stitches that would then form a chain-like pattern.

Chs

Chs simply stands for chains.

Ch-

This stands for space, or chain. This stands for the space between your stitches, or when there is a chain between the stitches and you couldn't work other stitches on them.

Ch sp

Ch sp means Chain Space, or the space between the chains you have on your pattern.

DC

┬ DC simply stands for double crochet, which means that you have to crochet twice.

Dc2tog

⋏ This stands for 2 DC together in 1 stitch, which means you have to crochet over 1 stitch twice.

Dec

Dec simply means to decrease the number of stitches you're doing.

Dtr

Dtr stands for Double Treble Crochet. This means that this is just a basic   crochet stitch that you can do by yarning over the hook thrice, and to draw 2 hoops at least 4 times.

Fo

FO stands for finished object, which means you're done with a certain pattern or so.

Foll

Foll stands for follow, which means you have to follow through with your stitches.

Fp

Fp means front post, which means you have to make crochet stitches on the front side of your fabric.

Fpdc

This stands for front post double crochet, which means that you have to make double crochet stitches

Fpsc

Fpsc stands for front post single crochet. In short, you have to make single stitches on the front side of your fabric.

Fptc

Fptc stands for front post treble crochet, which means you have to make treble stitches on the front side of your fabric.

G

G stands for gram, which is one of the measurements used for yarn, and the like.

HDC

HDC stands for half double crochet, or the means of doing just half of those double crochet stitches that you used to do.

in

in stands for inches (characterized by ").

Inc

Inc means increase. This means that you have to increase the number of stitches you're doing.

Incl

Incl stands for include, which means you have to include a certain thread, or type of stitch, into your project.

Lp

Lp stands for loop, which basically means that you have to loop a stitch.

M

M stands for mesh or meter.

Mc

Mc stands for main color, which is the main color you should use for your project.

Oz

Oz stands for ounce, another measurement used in terms of crocheting.

P

P stands for picot, which are stitches created by having the stitches chained together, and then creating slip stitches on the indicated space in your pattern.

Pat

Pat simply stands for pattern.

Pm

Pm stands for Place Marker, or the item that you use to mark the spot where you're at in your pattern.

Pc

Pc stands for popcorn. Popcorn stitches are rounded or compact oval stitches that are known to stand out of the fabric. Doing this takes time, but most crochet experts say that the finished product is actually worth it.

Rem

Rem is short for remaining, which is used to indicate the remaining number of stitches you still have to make on your fabric.

Rep

Rep stands for repeat, which tells you to repeat the kind of stitches you already made in a certain part of your fabric.

Rib

Rib means you have to create ribbing stitches. Ribbing stitches are stitches that are single-knit alongside single purl stitches, that you need to cast on your fabric to create.

Rs

Rs means right side, or the right side of your fabric.

RSC

RSC stands for Reverse Single Crochet, which basically means you have to create a certain stitch again in reverse.

Rnd

Rnd means round stitches.

Rnds

Rnds stands for a series of round stitches.

SC

✝ ✕ SC stands for single crochet, and are often symbolized by the given symbols above.

Sc2tog

Sc2tog means you have to create single crochet by weaving 2 stitches together.

Sc3tog

Sc3tog means you have to create a single crochet by weaving 3 stitches together.

Shl

Shl stands for shell, which is a series of stitches meant to look like a shell, and is often deemed to be one of the most beautiful and decorative stitches out there.

Sk

Sk means you have to skip some stitches.

Sl st

Sl St stands for slip stitch.

St

St simply stands for stitch.

Sts

Sts stands for stitches.

Sp

Sp means space, or the space between each of your stitches.

Sps

Sps means spaces.

Tbl

Tbl means through the back loop, or creating a stitch that would pass through the back of the loop.

Tog

Tog means together, or creating stitches that would come together.

T-chain

T-chain stands for turning stitches, or chains that start with the same height as the row of stitches you are working on.

 Tr stands for triple or treble crochet.

Tr Tr

 These are triple treble crochet stitches.

Ufo

Ufo doesn't have anything to do with aliens. On the contrary, it stands for an unfinished object—something that you have to leave as is on your fabric.

V-st

 These are basically just stitches shaped like the letter V.

WPI

WPI stands for the number of wraps per inch that you have to make.

WS

WS stands for Wrong Side, or the wrong side of the fabric that you have to work on.

YO

Yo stands for Yarn Over, or the act of threading yarn over some of your stitches.

Reading Diagrams

Another thing you need to know is that crocheting does not only deal with patterns, it also deals with diagrams. Some people think that diagrams are confusing, but for some, diagrams are deemed to be more helpful than patterns.

What you have to know is that diagrams are mostly used for repeating stitch patterns, creating borders, and even for edging. They're also used to demonstrate differences between patterns, too.

Row Diagrams

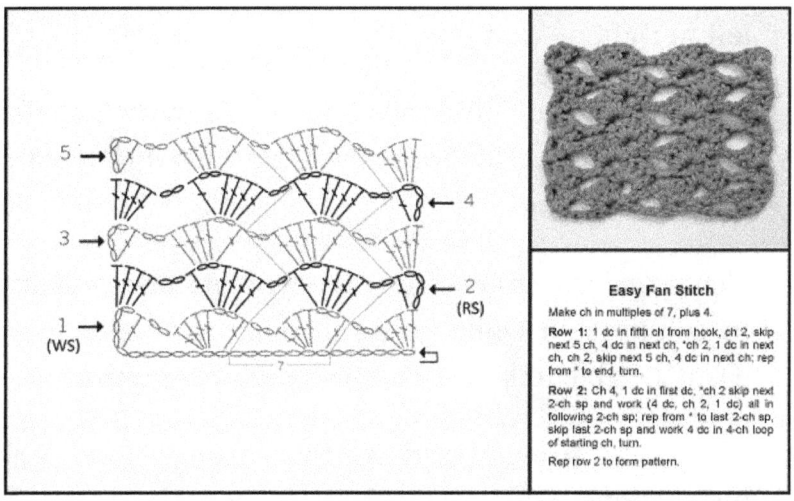

Easy Fan Stitch

Make ch in multiples of 7, plus 4.

Row 1: 1 dc in fifth ch from hook, ch 2, skip next 5 ch, 4 dc in next ch, *ch 2, 1 dc in next ch, ch 2, skip next 5 ch, 4 dc in next ch; rep from * to end, turn.

Row 2: Ch 4, 1 dc in first dc, *ch 2 skip next 2-ch sp and work (4 dc, ch 2, 1 dc) all in following 2-ch sp; rep from * to last 2-ch sp, skip last 2-ch sp and work 4 dc in 4-ch loop of starting ch, turn.

Rep row 2 to form pattern.

The first type of diagram you have to know about is the Row Diagram. Of course, you could keep in mind that this is used to create rows. Here's what you need to know about them:

1. These diagrams should be followed from the bottom all the way to the top. Mostly, they're designed for right handed crocheters; however, there are some patterns that are also meant for left-handed ones. If this is the case, it is indicated in the pattern.

2. You'll know where to go next by means of following the solid arrows you see on the pattern. Mostly, you start with a straight chain, and then you continue in zigzag motion, which means you'll have to work back and forth the pattern.

3. On the right side of the diagram, you'll find the number for the right side row. This means that you have to work left to right on that line.

4. Meanwhile, you'll find the wrong side row on the left side of the diagram. This means you have to work from right to left on this one.

5. Now, you have to make sure that your stitches will appear in columns so while going through the pattern, you'd easily be able to know where you have to go next.

6. There are some diagrams that also include written instructions. You'll find these instructions exactly at the

beginning of the pattern. Basically, these are just "x", "y", and their multiples.

7. To see which parts of the pattern you should repeat, take note of the bracketed or highlighted stitches you'd see on the pattern. They'll also indicate the number of stitches you have to repeat.

8. Hanging stitches, or chain stitches that hang just by the end of the row shall not be counted. However, you have to count a chain stitch that is situated directly above the row of stitches that you have.

Round Diagrams

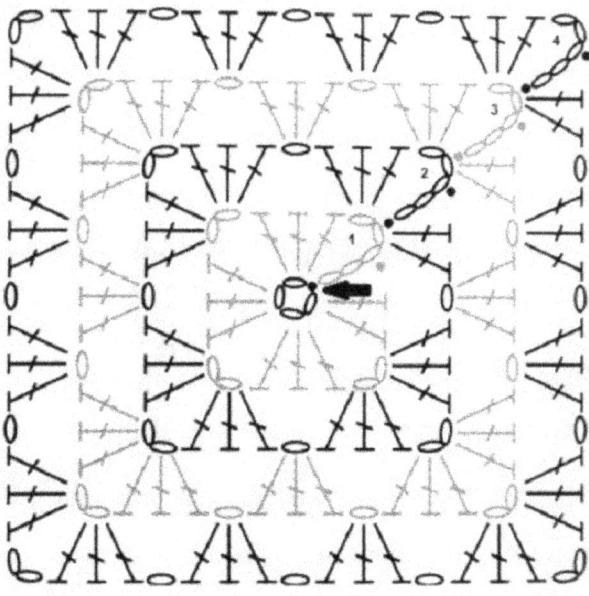

Round Diagrams mostly have rounded edges. Here's what you have to keep in mind about them:

1. First, you have to know where your starting point is. This is mainly what's in the center of the diagram, like what's shown above.

2. Remember not to turn your fabric over—not unless you read about it on the pattern. This will only make you confused, and would ruin the quality of your work.

3. Alternating colors and numbers determine different kinds of rounds.

4. What's frustrating about this, though, is that you would not know whether you should create more stitches, or work on chain stitches. Always refer to the written pattern.

When you see instructions in a bracket [ ] or a parentheses ( ) in your chosen pattern, it means that you need to repeat the instructions inside. There are patterns that specifically tell you up to how many times you need to do the instruction inside the bracket or parenthesis, and there are patterns that allow you to keep repeating the steps (while increasing or decreasing the number of stitches) according to your preference.

There are some patterns that use asterisk (*) to prompt a crocheter that a certain step needs to be repeated. The asterisk usually comes with a number which indicates the number of times that you need to repeat the instruction inside the brackets or parenthesis.

Memorize everything by heart and it will flow naturally.

CHAPTER 2

Your Materials and Tools

Gathering the materials and tools that you will need won't take so much of your time. It is recommended to start with a G or H hook size and light yarn category. In this chapter, you will see a chart for the different yarn as well as the right hook size to use. You will also see a chart for the different sizes of crocheting hook.

Take note that if your stitches are too tight or too loose, then your finished project might be slightly different from that of the pattern. If you have tight stitches, you can choose a bigger hook size, and smaller hook size if you have loose stitches – for now. Try to produce even stitches that are not too tight or too loose. Practice makes perfect, and you will surely enjoy every minute of it.

Here are those materials and tools that you need.

Your Yarn or Thread

Crochet yarns come in different categories and thickness, and you need to use the correct hook size according to the thickness of your thread or yarn. You are only allowed to use a bigger or smaller hook size if you still have tight or loose stitches. There are patterns that look gorgeous in a particular thickness of yarn, and look crappy if you use other yarn.

Each ball of yarn comes with a crochet gauge that indicates the number of stitches that you need to make in a number of inches (usually four). In the given chart below, the one used is two instead of four. Assuming that you followed the right hook size to use and the given number was far off the number of stitches on the crochet gauge, it only means that you have a problem with the tension of your stitches.

If you have more stitches than the number of stitches indicated on the crochet gauge, then your stitches are too tight. To create balance, you can use a bigger hook size than the one suggested.

If you have fewer stitches than the number of stitches on the crochet gauge, then your stitches are too loose. You need to use a smaller hook.

Almost always, the crochet gauge and the hook size are printed on the yarn label. It is recommended that you choose a cheaper yarn as your practice yarn. It is prudent to choose cheaper yarn since you are still on the learning stage. It is equally wise to choose light colored yarns; you will clearly see your error (just in case) and make necessary adjustments.

The chart below can help you understand and give you an idea about the different crochet threads and hook size to use.

Various Types of Yarn

As mentioned earlier, there are various types of yarn that you'll see in the market. Here's what you need to know about them.

Lace

Lace Yarn is characterized by being smooth, and silky, and is also known to be extremely fine. Often it is used for delicate crafts. It is also best for threading, and making really intricate details.

Thickness: 36 to 40 wpi

Gauge: 2 inches make 17 to 20 stitches

Metric Hook Size: 1.5mm to 2.25mm

U.S. Hook Size: B (aluminum)/ No. 4 or 6 (steel)

English Hook Size: 14 (aluminum)/ No. 2 or 2.5 (steel)

Fine

Fine Yarn is usually used for baby and sports garments, such as pullovers, sandal socks, mittens, and jerseys.

Thickness: 15 to 18 wpi

Gauge: 2 inches make 8 to 10 stitches

Metric Hook Size: 3.5 mm to 4.5 mm

U.S. Hook Size: E, F, G, H, I (aluminum)

English Hook Size: 6, 7, 8, or 9 (aluminum)

Super Fine

Super Fine Yarn is usually used for making wraps, shawls, socks, and other baby items. It's also sometimes called baby or sock yarn.

Thickness: 19 to 22 wpi

Gauge: 2 inches make 11 to 16 stitches

Metric Hook Size: 2.25 to 3.5mm

U.S. Hook Size: C, D, or E (aluminum)

English Hook Size: 9, 11, or 12 (aluminum)

Light

Just like Fine Yarn, Light Yarn is also often used to make baby clothes, and socks. It's also generally used to make other types of lightweight clothing, too.

Thickness: 11 to 14 wpi

Gauge: 2 inches make 6 to 9 stitches

Metric Hook Size: 4.5 mm to 5.5 mm

U.S. Hook Size: G, H, I (aluminum)

English Hook Size: 5, 6, or 7 (lightweight aluminum)

Medium

Thickness: 9 to 11 wpi

Gauge: 2 inches make 6 to 7 stitches

Metric Hook Size: 5.5mm to 6.5mm

U.S. Hook Size: I or J (aluminum)

English Hook Size: 4 or 5 (aluminum)

Bulky

Bulky Yarn is used to make most winter items, such as scarves and hats. It's also essential for making home décor, and other bulky-weight super-washes.

Thickness: 8 to 9 wpi

Gauge: 2 inches make 4 to 6 stitches

Metric Hook Size: 6.5mm to 9mm

U.S. Hook Size: K (aluminum)

English Hook Size: 1/0, 2, or 2/0 (aluminum)

Super Bulky

Thickness: 7 to 8 wpi

Gauge: 2 inches make 3 to 5 stitches

Metric Hook Size: 9mm and larger

U.S. Hook Size: P (aluminum)

English Hook Size: 2/0 or 3/0 (aluminum)

Wraps per inch, or wpi, is the number of thread strands that can be lined side by side within one inch. If you have an unknown ball of yarn lying around or has no label to give you information regarding the kind of thickness, then you can do the wpi test. Wrap the yarn around the ruler; count the number of strands you get in one inch. Make sure not to wrap tightly. The strands should be lined properly without overlapping. There should be no gaps between the strands to get the right measurement. The number you will get can help you determine the thickness of the yarn.

How to Hold the Thread

The most ideal way to hold your thread (if you are right handed) is to take the free end of the thread and wind the thread clockwise once around the smallest finger of your left hand while your right hand holds the free end of the thread. Move the thread towards your index finger, and wrap it once around your index finger. Secure the free end of the thread using your thumb and middle finger.

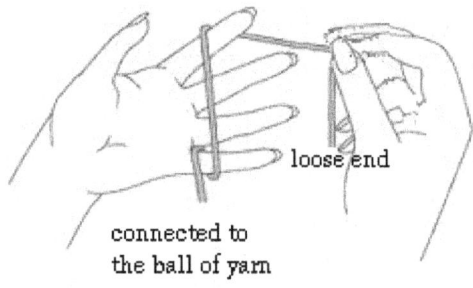

loose end

connected to
the ball of yarn

To understand the different hook sizes better, you will find the next topic useful. It will give you a quick view of how each hook looks like. Understand that different manufacturers have different styles and designs, but the appearance of the hook should remain the same.

Crochet Hook Size Chart

Here is a chart that can give you an idea of the kind of hook that you can use for each type of yarn. Just focus on the size of the hook (some shafts presented in the chart are longer or shorter than the actual); the shafts of the different hook sizes have the same lengths, depending on the manufacturer.

Crochet Hook Conversion Chart		
Metric	**USA**	**UK**
2.00 mm	-	14
2.25 mm	1 / B	13
2.50 mm	-	12
2.75 mm	C	11
3.00 mm	-	11
3.25 mm	D	10
3.50 mm	4 / E	9
3.75 mm	F	-
4.00 mm	6	8
4.25 mm	G	-
4.50 mm	7	7
5.00 mm	8 / H	6
5.50 mm	9 / I	5
6.00 mm	10 / J	4
6.50 mm	10 1/2 / K	3
7.00 mm	-	2
8.00 mm	-	0
9.00 mm	15 / N	00
10.00 mm	P	000
15.75 mm or 16mm	Q	-

Steel Hook Chart (thread hooks)		
Metric	**USA**	**UK**
.6 mm	14	6
.75 mm	13	-
.70 mm	12	5
.8 mm	11	-
1 mm	10	4
1.15 mm	9	-
1.25 mm	8	3
1.50 mm	7	2.5
1.6 mm	6	-
1.7 mm	5	-
1.75 mm	4	2
1.85 mm	3	-
1.95 mm	2	-
2 mm	1	1
2.25 mm	0	00
3 mm	00	-

Steel and aluminum are the usual materials for the hook. There are some crochet hooks that come in bamboo, plastic, and combinations of the different materials. You can choose any hook material, but just make sure that you choose the hook with a nice hold.

There are cheap crochet hooks and there are expensive crochet hooks with fancy designs, but it is best to start with a cheap hook. Get a more expensive one later.

Choosing your Crochet Hook

As mentioned before, a novice should choose the F, G, H, or I U.S. hook size, and fine to medium thread. Look at the crochet hook size chart to see the different hook sizes and their material. First, take a detour in learning the proper way to hold your hook and the different grips.

The Pencil Grip

Finding the right grip that you are comfortable with is important because it allows you to work with ease and make crocheting more enjoyable. The pencil grip is the more favored grip between the two types of grip. Just as the name suggests, the pencil grip lets you hold your hook as if you're holding a pencil. This grip can give you maximum control when crocheting as you are writing. It gives the same feeling when you write on a paper using your pencil. This grip gives a natural flow each time you hook a yarn.

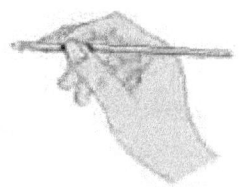

pencil grip

The Knife Grip

There are some who find it easy to crochet using the knife grip and feels more comfortable using the said grip. In a knife grip, you hold your crochet hook in the same manner that you hold a knife. It is an overhand grip that gives you the same ease and control as slicing something using a knife.

knife grip

More people favor pencil grip, but only you can tell which grip suits your preference – the one that can give you comfort and ease.

Types of Crochet Hooks

So, you've seen the chart, and the grips. But what really are these hooks about, and what else should you know about them? Read on and find out!

1. **Aluminum.** Aluminum Hooks are quite flexible. They are available in a vast amount of sizes, and make crocheting quick, and smooth!

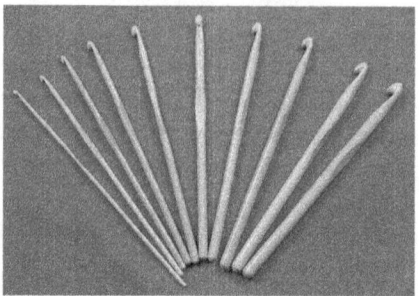

2. **Steel.** Steel Hooks are known to be best used for small objects, and are often partnered with fine thread. Steel hooks are also known as thread hooks. Examples of crafts you could make with them include doilies, and handkerchiefs.

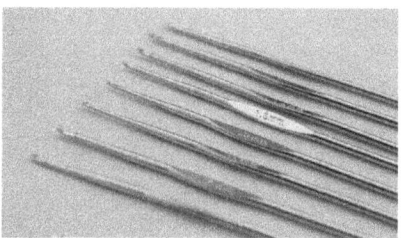

3. **Bamboo.** Meanwhile, bamboo hooks are known to be warm and lightweight. They could either be small, or large, never in between.

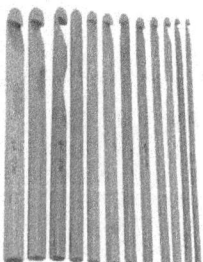

4. **Plastic.** Plastic Hooks could often be common sized or jumbo. They're usually made with plastic that's hollow, and are also lightweight.

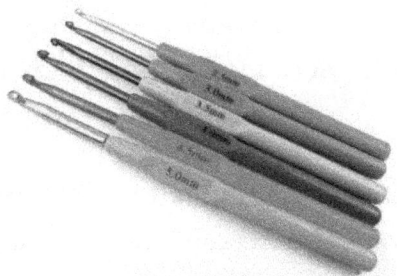

5. **Tunisian.** Finally, you have Tunisian Hooks. They're longer than regular hooks. Sometimes, Tunisian Hooks are called Cro Hooks. They're known for having hooks on both ends, and that's why they're sometimes not recommended for beginners. Tunisian Hooks are usually used to make crafts that are in the same mechanism as knitted projects. This means that the fabric doesn't look the same as normal crocheted projects do. This is because the stitches stay on the hook while you're making the project, instead of being on the canvas itself.

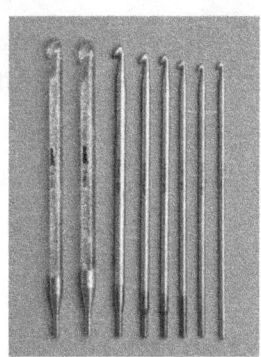

Things to Remember

1. Remember that crochet hook sizes are not universal. This is why you have metric, U.S., and English sizes, and others, too. Remember that size always depends on the country where the hooks were made, the brand, and the material, as well.

2. Size is often determined by the shaft's diameter. The shaft is the point between the needle, and the hook. This will then help you understand how big your stitches shall be.

3. Best thing to keep in mind about size is that hooks made in the United States are represented by letters in their sizes. The farther the letter in the alphabet, the larger the hooks get.

4. Remember that steel hooks best work with lace thread. Take note that as the number gets smaller, the hooks get larger.

Tapestry Needle

There are projects that require you to sew your work, and you will need a tapestry needle for that. You can also use the tapestry needle to sew a crocheted appliqué to your project if it can make the project more appealing. The needle is typically larger than the average needle for sewing and has a rounded (blunt) tip. It has a threading eye to accommodate any yarn, although it may not work for bulky threads.

While often used for cross-stitching, tapestry needles prove to be useful for crocheted materials, too, especially if you need to put on more detail on your project.

Pictured above are various Tapestry Needle sizes. (L-R: 28, 26, 24, 22, 20, 18, 16)

As you may have noticed, the larger the needle, the smaller the number gets—so don't get confused into buying a largely numbered needle thinking it would be a small-sized one.

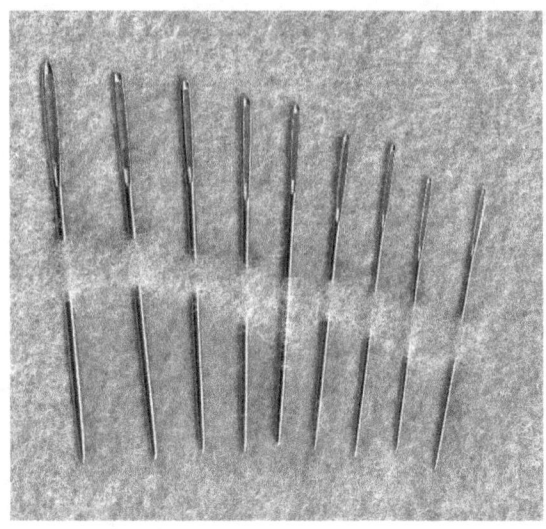

(L-R: 18, 19, 20, 21, 22, 23, 24, 25, 26)

Meanwhile, there are also other tapestry needles called *Tweens*. These are needles that fall between tapestry needles of regular sizes. Tweens are best used for projects where regular sized ones may be a little too small or large.

Choosing Tapestry Needles

Now, you may wonder how exactly you'd choose your tapestry needles. Well, general rule of thumb here is to make sure that you use the kind of needles that will easily accommodate whatever yarn or thread you're currently working with. This means that you'd have to use the smallest needle available, but not necessarily the smallest one out of all sizes, because this would do nothing good for your fabric.

Scissors

To give your thread a clean cut, you need a pair of scissors. It does not need to be an expensive pair, just the one that is sharp enough to cut your thread without trouble. Make sure to maintain your scissors properly.

As for crochet scissors, one of the most recommended ones are Stork Embroidery Scissors. They're amazing because they do not leave unhinged threads on your project, and would definitely make your crafts neat as could be. Even stitches in front of your fabric will be neatly removed.

A sample is shown below.

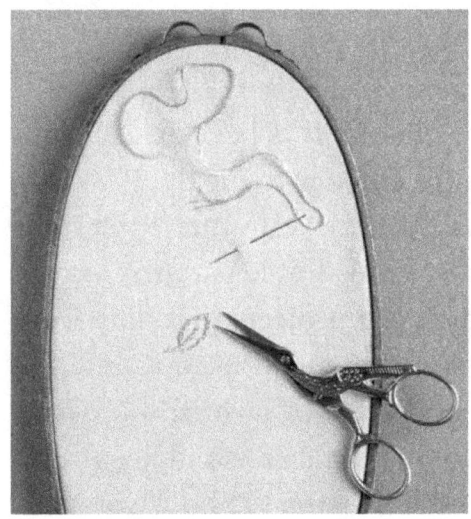

Stitch Markers

The usual stitch markers look like key holders, paper clips, small plastic hoops, and tiny padlocks. The markers are useful in keeping track of the start or end of a round in the pattern with repetitive instructions. The marker can also serve as reminder of the number of stitches that you made so far. You can also use the markers to keep track of the round that you are currently crocheting.

You can use improvised markers like pieces of thread that you can loosely tie around the post of your stitches on your current round, safety pins, and/or plastic rings. You can use different combinations of materials to mark different rounds

Crochet Hook Case

Your most important tool is your hook. It is best to keep your hook inside a case to avoid possible damage to the tip. It is quite difficult to maneuver your hook the way you want if the tip is bent. There will also come a time when simple patterns are not enough to hone your craft. There are projects that only work well with a certain type of yarn and you will need a different hook for that. You might even find yourself owning more than two hooks and you need to store them in a case and keep them organized. You will have no trouble picking the hook you need if you have them in a case.

Now, it's time to learn the basic stitches and perhaps more.

CHAPTER 3

The Different Basic Stitches of Crochet

This is where the fun begins. You will learn all the basic stitches that most crochet patterns require.

The Slip Knot

Create a pretzel with your yarn (see the illustration).

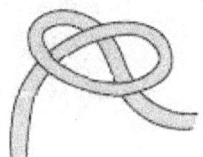

Look at the illustration below and try to copy the position of the hook to create a knot.

You need to produce this:

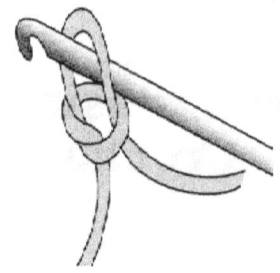

Now you have a slip knot.

How to Yarn Over

Yarn over is simply wrapping the yarn over the hook. You need to yarn over each time you make a stitch. You can yarn over before inserting your hook to the next stitch or after inserting your hook to the next stitch – depending on the kind of stitch you are making.

You do a yarn over each time you wrap a thread around the shaft of your hook and through the stitch (see figure below).

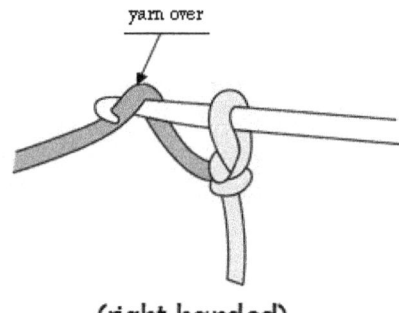

(right handed)

Chain Stitch (ch)

A crochet project will always have chain stitches for a base. You need to produce even chain stitches to come up with a quality work.

Make a slip knot and secure the knot between your thumb and middle finger. Hook a thread or yarn over (see above figure) and slip it through the stitch. Now you have your first chain stitch. Take note that the slip knot is not regarded as a chain stitch and should not be included in the count. Loosen the ball of yarn as you increase the number of your chain stitches.

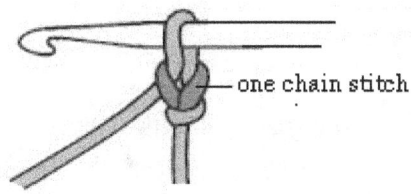

one chain stitch

Do more chain stitches to make a line. You need to practice this stitch before proceeding to the next lesson. You are not expected to get even stitches right away, but you are expected to practice while having fun.

Take a look at the figure below to understand the parts that are not considered part of a series of chain stitches.

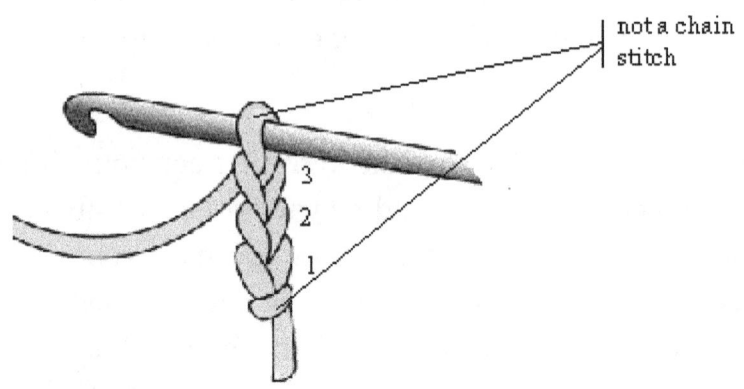

not a chain stitch

Slip Stitch (sl st)

Slip stitch is usually what you can call a "closer" stitch because it joins the two ends of your chain stitch series to form a circle. It can also join two crocheted components together.

Make a series of chain stitches first. To make a slip stitch, you need to insert your hook (with a loop, see left figure below) through a stitch that is farther from you and now you have two loops around your hook (see right figure below).

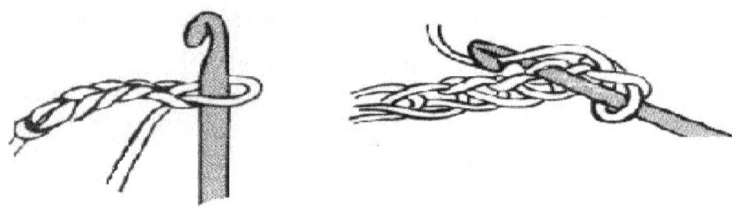

Yarn over and pull the hooked thread through the two loops (see left figure below). You should get one slip stitch and a single loop around your hook (see right figure).

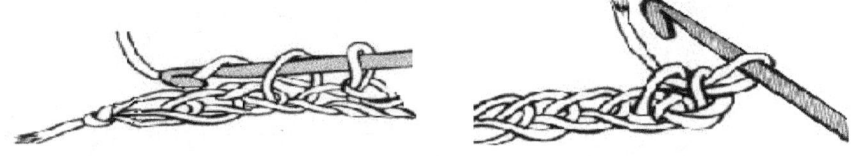

Before jumping to the next lesson, let yourself get acquainted first with turning chain. Each round in a crochet pattern requires a turning chain. A turning chain usually starts a new round and it also serves as the first stitch of that round. If you need 5 treble crochet, you should have 1 turning chain plus 4 treble crochet.

Turning Chain

The turning chain is always the first stitch each time you start another round. When the next round starts with a slip stitch, then you don't need a turning chain and it is the only stitch where a turning chain is not needed.

The height of the different basic stitches varies, and your turning chain should have the same height as the stitch being asked by the pattern. See the figure below as your reference.

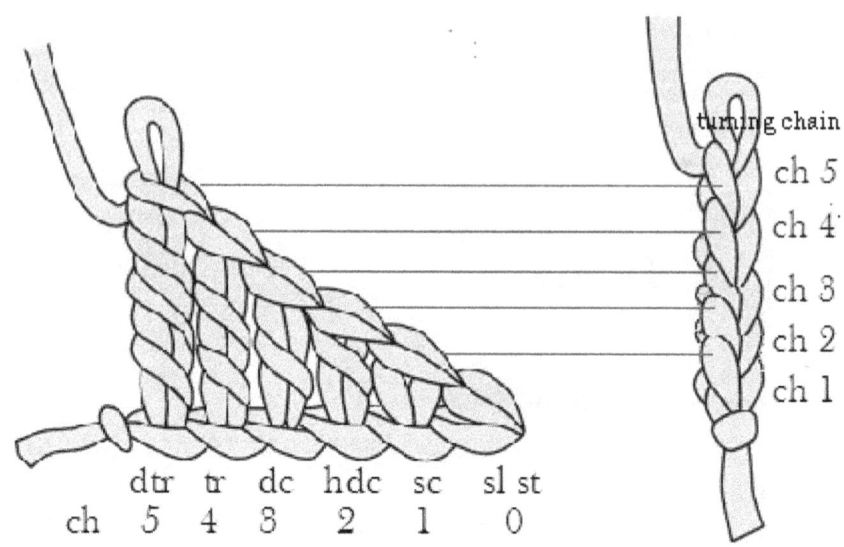

Slip stitch does not require a turning chain.

Single crochet needs 1 chain stitch as turning chain.

Half double crochet needs 2 chain stitches as turning chain.

Double crochet needs 3 chain stitches as turning chain.

Treble crochet needs 4 chain stitches as turning chain.

Double treble crochet needs 5 chain stitches as turning chain.

If you are working in rows (not in circle), make sure to always turn your work in the same direction (see figure 1) when adding a row. If you started turning your work to the right, then see to it to always turn your work to the right each time you add a row. Proceed with your work (see figure 2).

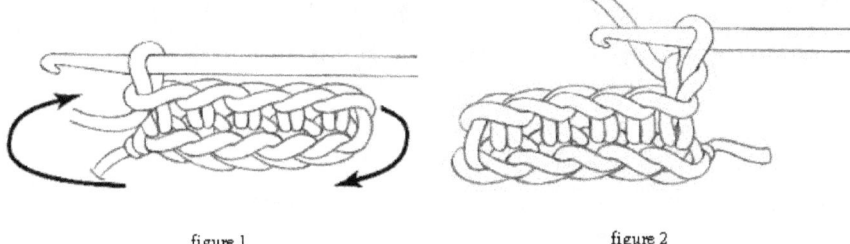

figure 1   figure 2

Single Crochet (sc)

Make 11 chain stitches as base.

1. Slip your hook into the 2nd chain (see below).

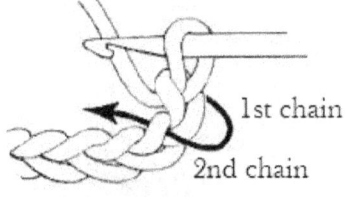

1st chain

2nd chain

2. Yarn over and hook the thread through the same chain. You now have two loops around your hook.

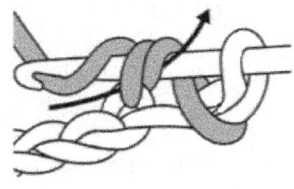

3. Yarn over once more and hook the thread through the two loops around your hook. You have a single crochet stitch.

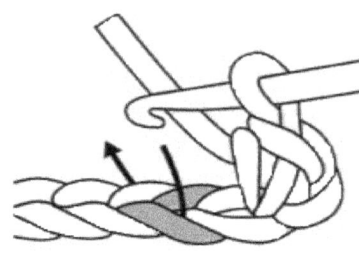

4. Slip your hook into the next chain and yarn over. Hook the thread through the same chain and you should have two loops around your hook.

5. Do steps 3 and 4 again, and do this up to the last chain.

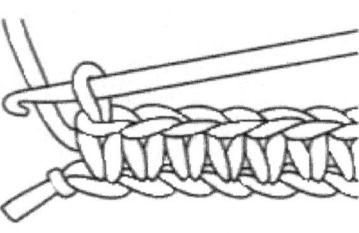

You can make a longer base chain if you want to practice more.

Half Double Crochet (hdc)

Make 12 chain stitches as base.

1. Yarn over to produce two loops around your hook. Insert your hook into the 3rd chain (see below).

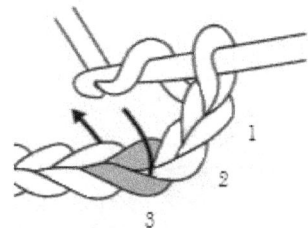

2. Yarn over and hook a thread through the same chain. You now have three loops around your hook.

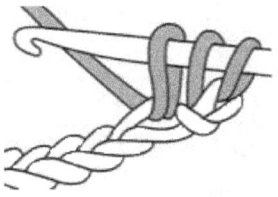

3. Yarn over and hook the thread through the three loops. Now you have a half double crochet stitch.

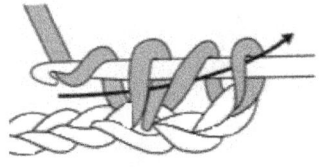

4. Yarn over to produce two loops around your hook. Slip your hook into the next chain, yarn over, and hook a thread through that same chain. You now have three loops around your hook.

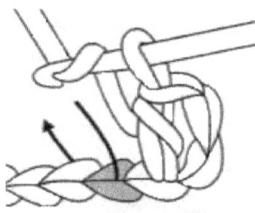

5. Do steps 3 and 4 again, and keep doing this up to the last chain.

Double Crochet (dc)

Make 13 chain stitches as base.

1. Yarn over and you have two loops around your hook. Slip your hook into the 4th chain.

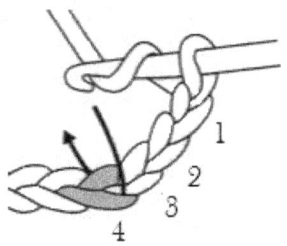

2. Yarn over and hook a thread through the same chain. You now have three loops around your hook.

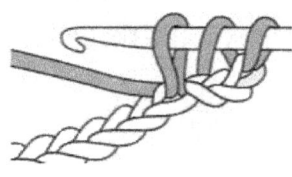

3. Yarn over and hook a thread through the two loops around the hook and there will still be two loops left. Yarn over again, and hook a thread through the remaining two loops. You now have a double crochet.

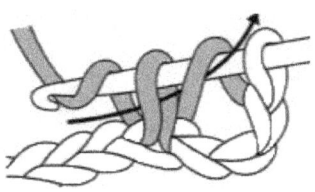 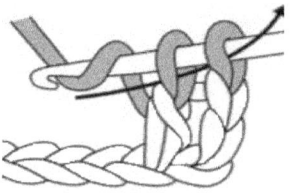

4. Yarn over and you have two loops around your hook. Slip your hook into the next chain, yarn over, and hook a thread through the same chain. You should produce three loops around your hook.

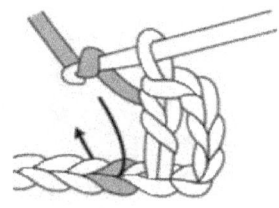

5. Do steps 3 and 4 once more, and keep repeating down to the last chain.

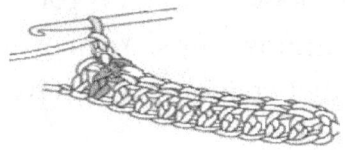

Treble or Triple Crochet (tr)

Make 14 chain stitches as base.

1. Yarn over twice and you have three loops around your hook. Slip your hook into the 5th chain.

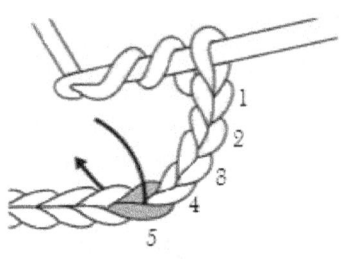

2. Yarn over and hook a thread through the same chain. You should produce four loops around your hook.

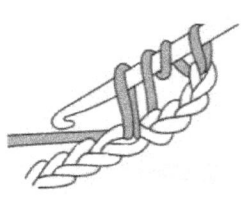

3. Yarn over and hook a thread through the two loops around the hook and you still have three loops left around your hook. Yarn over again, and hook a thread through the two loops and there will be two remaining loops. Yarn over, and hook a thread through the remaining two loops. You have a treble crochet.

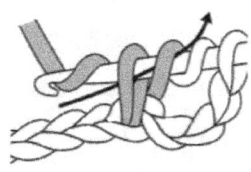 

4. Yarn over twice and you will have three loops around your hook. Insert your hook into the next chain, and do step 2.

5. Keep doing steps 3 and 4 to the last chain.

Treble or Triple Crochet (tr)

Make 14 chain stitches as base.

1. Yarn over twice and you have three loops around your hook. Slip your hook into the 5th chain.

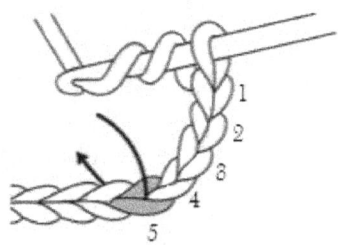

2. Yarn over and hook a thread through the same chain. You should produce four loops around your hook.

3. Yarn over and hook a thread through the two loops around the hook and you still have three loops left around your hook. Yarn over again, and hook a thread through the two loops and there are two remaining loops. Yarn over, and hook a thread through the remaining two loops. You have a treble crochet.

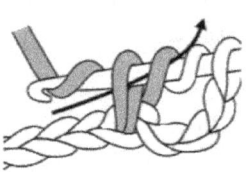 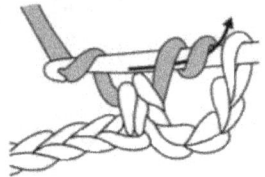

4. Yarn over twice and you will have three loops on your hook. Insert your hook into the next chain, and do step 2.

5. Keep doing steps 3 and 4 to the last chain.

Double Treble Crochet (dtr)

Make 15 chain stitches as base.

1. Yarn over three times and you have four loops around your hook. Insert your hook into the 6th chain.

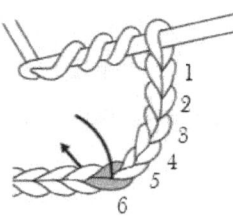

2. Yarn over and hook a thread through the same chain. You should produce five loops around your hook.

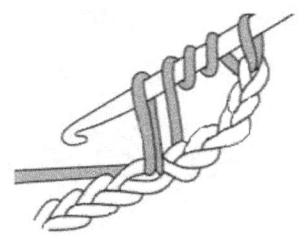

3. Yarn over and hook a thread through the two loops around the hook and four loops still remain around your hook. Yarn over again, and hook a thread through the two loops, and three loops still remain around your hook. Yarn over, and hook a thread through the two loops, and two loops still remain around you hook. Yarn over for the last time, and hook a thread through the two loops and you will get a double treble crochet stitch.

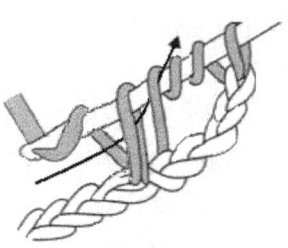

4. Yarn over thrice and you have four loops around your hook. Insert your hook into the next chain, and do step 2.

5. Do steps 3 and 4 until there's no more base chain to work on.

Parts of the Crochet Stitch

Take note of the different parts of crochet stitch. There are patterns that require you to work only on the front or back loop.

There are also patterns that require you to do a back post or front post.

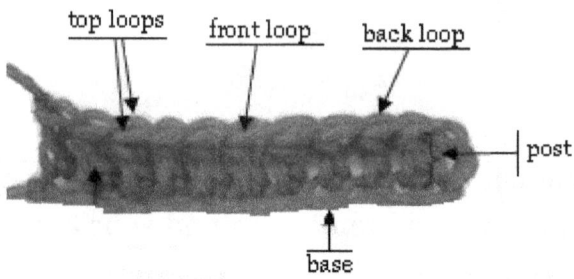

How to Work a Front Post

For this lesson, we will use dc to create fpdc. When you want to raise a crochet stitch, then you need to use front post stitches. Start where your double crochet lesson ended.

You have one row of finished dc stitches. Turn your work (see figure 1 under Turning Chain) and continue with the next row (see figure 2 under Turning Chain). Use ch-2 as your turning chain instead of 3. Fpdc stitches are shorter than the normal dc stitches.

Yarn over and slip your hook from front going to the back of the next post (the post beneath the row that you are currently working on) and to the front again.

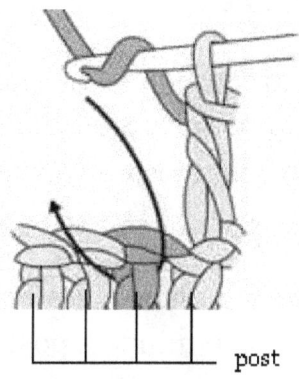

post

Hook a thread and lead it back to your starting position. You should have three loops around your hook.

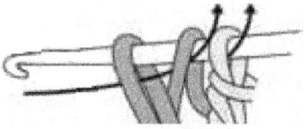

Yarn over, hook a thread, and slip it through the two loops around the hook. Do it twice.

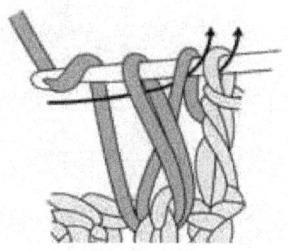

You can follow the same procedure for fpsc; you only need to use single crochet instead of double crochet.

How to Work a Back Post

Again, we will use dc to create bpdc. When you want to create the opposite effect of front post, then you need to use back post stitches. You can start from where your double crochet lesson has left off.

You already have a row of finished dc stitches. Turn your work (don't forget to look at the reminders posted on Turning Chain) and continue with the next row. Use ch-2 as your turning chain because bpdc stitches are shorter than normal dc stitches.

Yarn over and slip your hook from back going to the front of the next post (the same with front post, only in reverse) and to the back again.

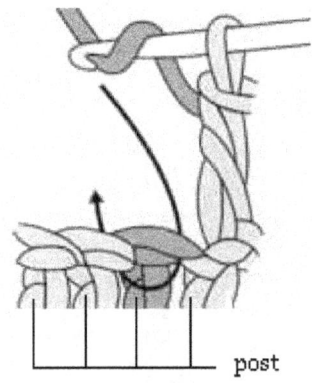

post

Hook a thread and guide it back to your initial position. You should produce three loops around your hook.

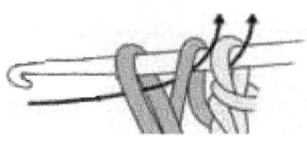

Yarn over, hook a thread, and slip it through the two loops around the hook. Do it twice.

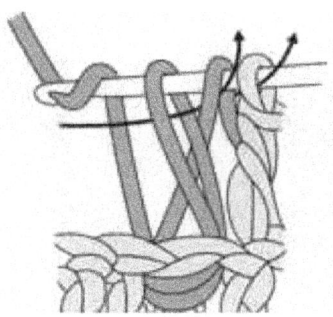

Follow the same procedure when working with bpsc; use single crochet instead of double crochet.

How to work a Picot Stitch

If you may recall, picot stitches are used to work on edges of finished items. They're also used to make detailed, beautiful stitches, and could also be turned into squares.

1. Make sure that you work exactly on the edge of a finished stitch.

2. Then, start single-crocheting in the first stitch, before crocheting in the next stitch, which would then be the third chain.

3. Then, go on and make more single crochets in the next 3 stitches to make the picot. Check it out below.

4. Then, repeat step 3 all across the row.

How to work the Seed Stitch

Seed Stitches are series of alternating double and single-crochet stitches, which would then give you a result of a closed stitch.

1. First, you have to start with a chain. Then, make a turn and start single-crocheting starting from the 2nd stitch you see on the hook.

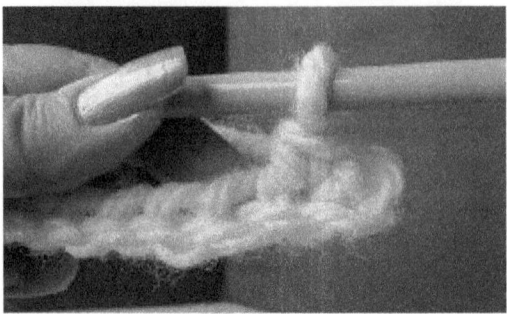

2. Now, the next thing you have to do for the next stitch is to make a double-crochet.

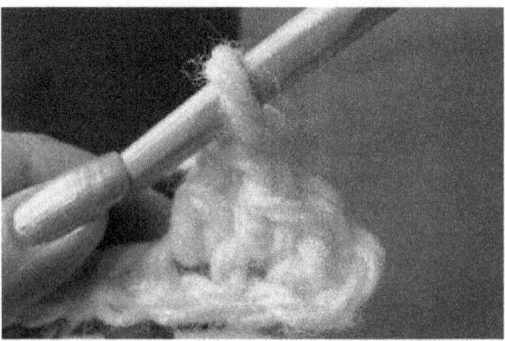

3. Then, for the next stitch, you have to single-crochet.

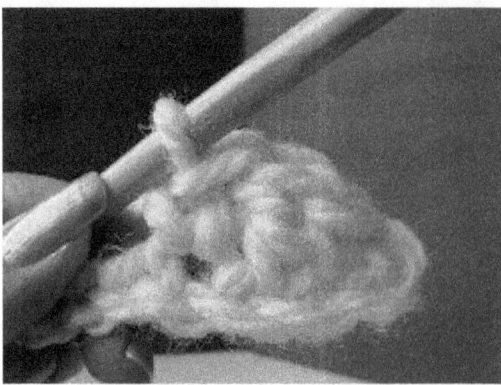

4. Across the row, all you'd have to do is repeat steps 2 and 3, to create a row of complete seed stitches.

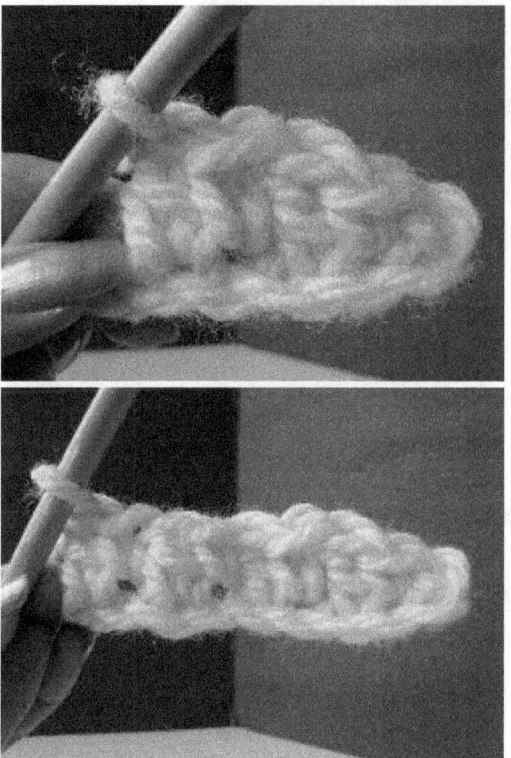

5. Now, once you reach the end of the row, it's time for you to turn what you're working on. If it ends on a single stitch, do a double stitch next, and vice versa.

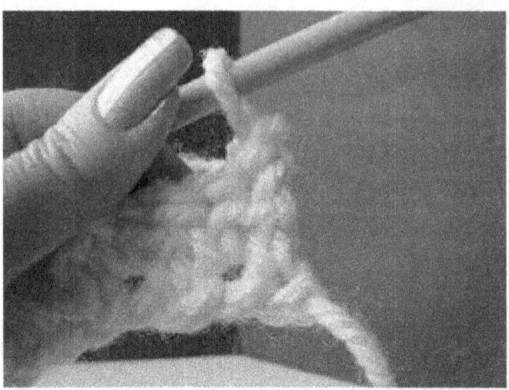

6. Make sure that you work your way through the row. Just repeat steps 2 to 3 until you reach your desired length and texture.

How to Crochet in the Round

Crocheting in the Round means you're going to stitch out your pattern. As a beginner, this is one of the most important things you could learn. Here's how.

1. First, you have to start chaining a ring. This will be your starting point. Make sure to chain 5, and then use a slip stitch for joining.

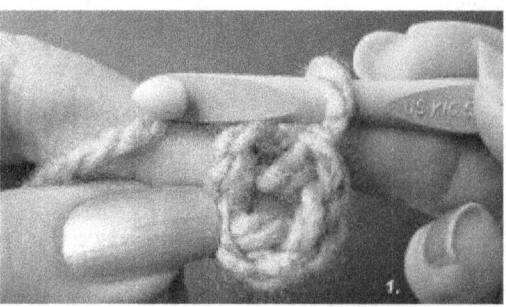

2. Next, start double crochet by making chain 2.

3. Now, check your pattern, and see how many double stitches you need for this round. For example, 10 double crochets would make chain 2.

4. Now, join the stitches together by making a slip stitch. Do this on top of the chain at the row's beginning.

5. It's now time to make the next round of stitches. For this, you'd have to do chain 2.

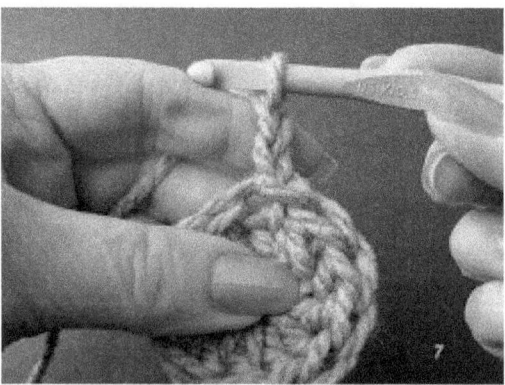

6. Now, you have to start working in the other direction. To do this, you have to turn your canvas. Just go on and continue working on the rest of the stitches.

7. Complete this round's needed number of stitches, and then join the round once more by making slip stitches.

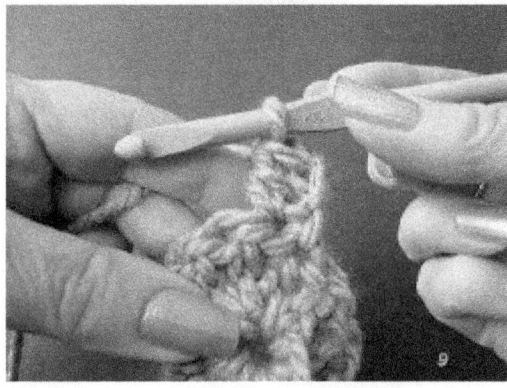

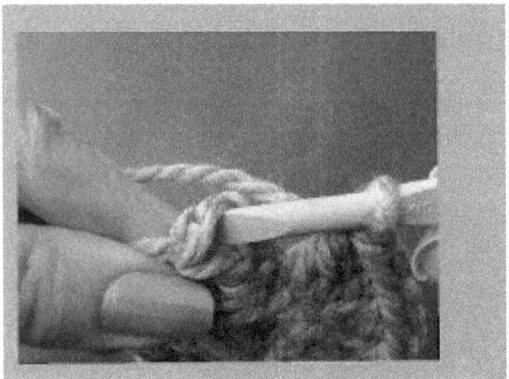

8. The arrow you see on the image below determines the position where you should make your slip stitches to keep the stitches joined together.

9. When you do it right, you'll get a perfect round-shaped object just like the one below:

How to work a Basketweave Stitch

One of the most interesting types of stitches out there, the Basketweave Stitch basically looks like a basket. Sometimes, it's also known as the Waffle Stitch. You'd use a lot of single and double crochet stitches here .

1. Make chain 22, or a foundation piece where you could then work on the rest of your stitches to complete the basketweave stitch.

2. From the 3rd stitch from the hook, start making double crochet stitches. Do this into each stitch of the chain.

3. Chain 2 and turn to make the front post stitch, and then yarn over and insert your hook over the previous row's double crochet stitches.

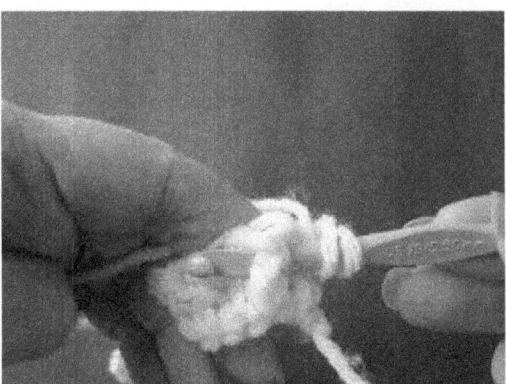

4. Repeat the process in the next 2 stitches that you're going to make so that you'd get a total of 4 front post stitches.

5. Then, do the back stitch post by inserting the hook behind the previous row's double crochet stitches, and then go and complete a double crochet.

6. Continue doing as you're told, and then when you see that you have reached the end of the row, make a chain 2, and then turn, and repeat making your double crochet stitches.

7. Whatever you have done on your earlier row, that's also what you have to do in the next row. (i.e., 4 stitches = 4 stitches). Continue doing so until you create the length of fabric you want.

How to work a Cable Stitch

Cable Stitches are meant to spruce up your work some more. It may seem complicated but the truth is this type of stitch only uses four core stitches to make. Here's how:

1. Start by chaining multiples of 4 stitches, then add 3 more. 16 stitches is equal to 4 cables. From the second row of the hook, go on and make single stitches. Do this for each part of the chain.

2. Next, make chain 3 and then turn your work before skipping the next stitch. Work on the next 3 stitches by double-crocheting.

3. Work from front to back by inserting your hook, and do it into the first stitch that you have skipped.

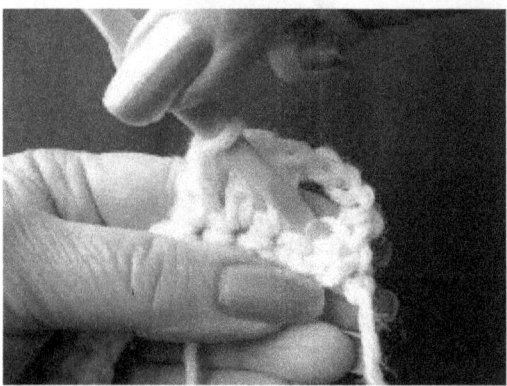

4. Then, loosely draw a loop and take it to the top of the last stitch that you have worked on. Do a yarn over to finish the stitch, and make sure it goes all the way through the loops.

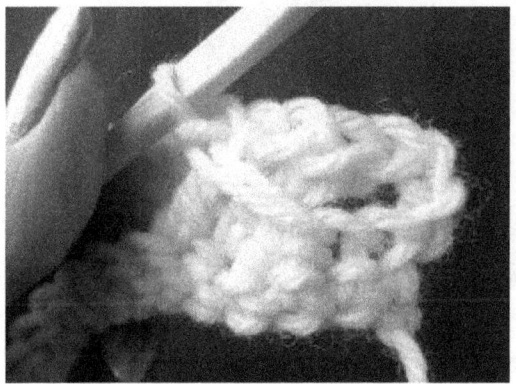

5. Repeat steps 1 to 4 all across the row, and then end with double crochet before chaining 1, and making a single crochet.

6. Repeat all the given steps once more to create something that resembles the one below:

How to work a Crazy Shell Stitch

A Crazy Shell stitch is your improved version of the Regular Shell stitch. It's one of the most beautiful stitches you could make, and could be used for decorative purposes.

1. First, you have to start with multiples of a chain. Try multiples of three, and make sure you add another one. For example, 9 plus 1, 12 plus 1, etc. Then, from the 4th stitch on the hook, make sure to make 3 double crochets.

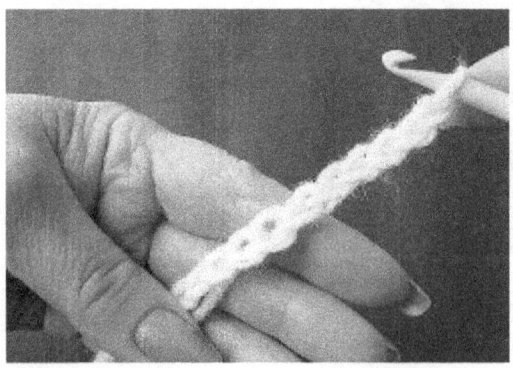

2. Then, single crochet on the 4th stitch. Make sure you do not do anything with the next 3 stitches from your starting point.

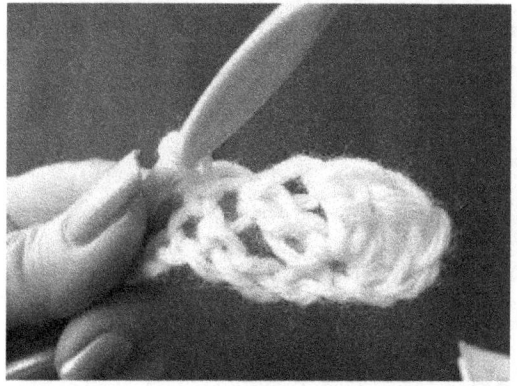

3. Then, chain 3, and make 3 double crochet in the same stitch. Then, skip the next 3 stitches again, and on the next stitch, make single crochet.

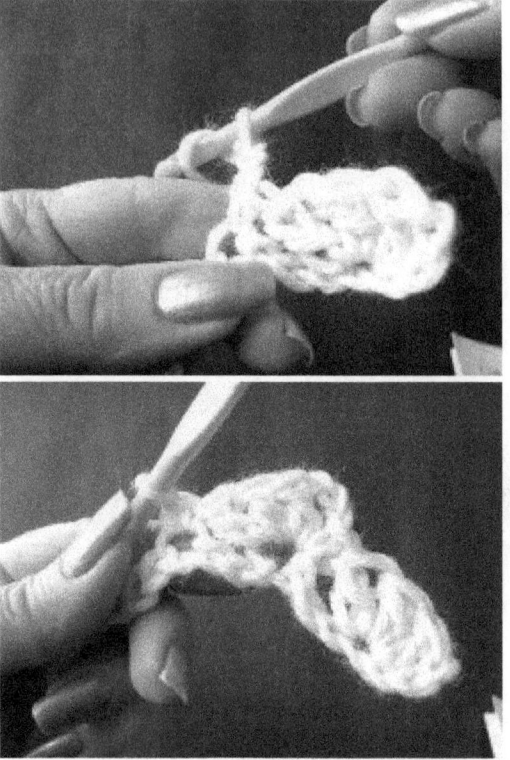

4. For the second row, make chain 3, and turn your work around. Now, make 3 double crochet in the previous row's single crochet, and then single crochet in the next chain 3 space.

5. Next, make double crochet stitches in the same space, and then single crochet in the next space. Repeat this all across the row.

6. Then, repeat this on the 2nd row and continue until you reach your desired shape and size.

How to work a Checkerboard Stitch

The Checkerboard Stitch is one of the neatest stitches out there. It's meant to crochet or dishcloth squares together, and is usually used to create afghans and the like.

1. First, you have to start with a chain. From the 3rd stitch on your hook, make a double crochet stitch, and repeat this on the next stitch, as well.

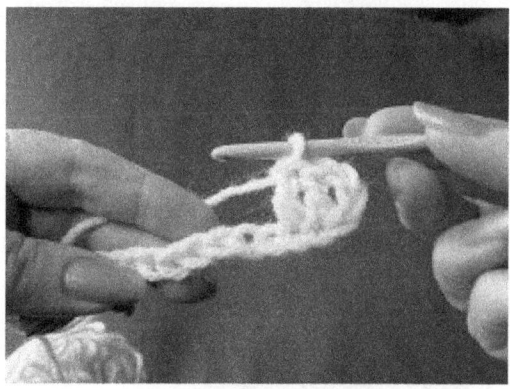

2. Then, create chain 3, and make sure to skip the next 3 stitches. Once you have done so, double crochet until the next 3 stitches.

3. Repeat the given steps above until you reach the end of your row. Make sure to end the last stitch with a double crochet.

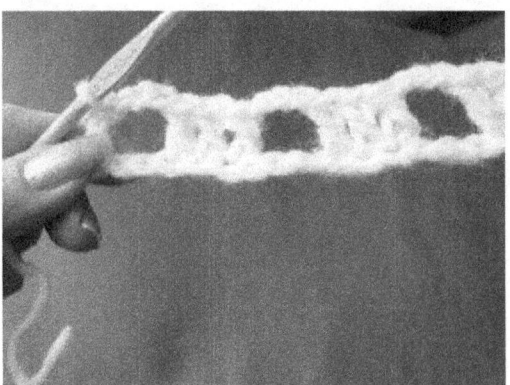

4. Next, make a chain 3, and then turn your work over. Then, make 2 double crochet stitches in the previous row's chain 3.

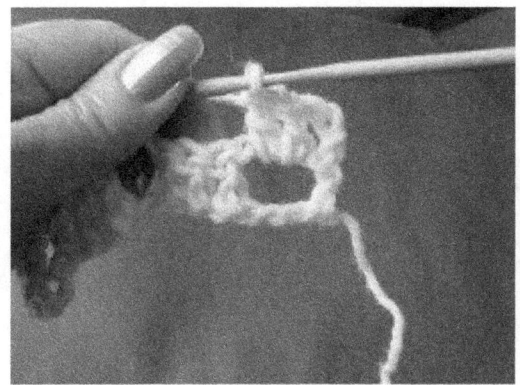

5. Next, you have to make another chain 3 and make sure to double crochet right in the space of the second row, where you have not made anything earlier.

6. Make sure to repeat all the steps towards the next row, and keep doing so until you reach your desired size and shape.

How to work a Popcorn Stitch

Popcorn Stitches may seem complicated but they're actually quite easy. Basically, you just need knowledge of double stitches!

1. First, you have to make sure that you have a foundation chain which you can then divide into three, and then go and single crochet the hook. Do this into each stitch of your chain.

2. Next, chain 1 and turn your work, then the next 2 stitches should be single-crocheted. Then, make 5 double stitches until you reach the last loop of the string.

3. Then, make slip stitches until you reach all 6 loops that you have, and then single crochet until the next 3 stitches.

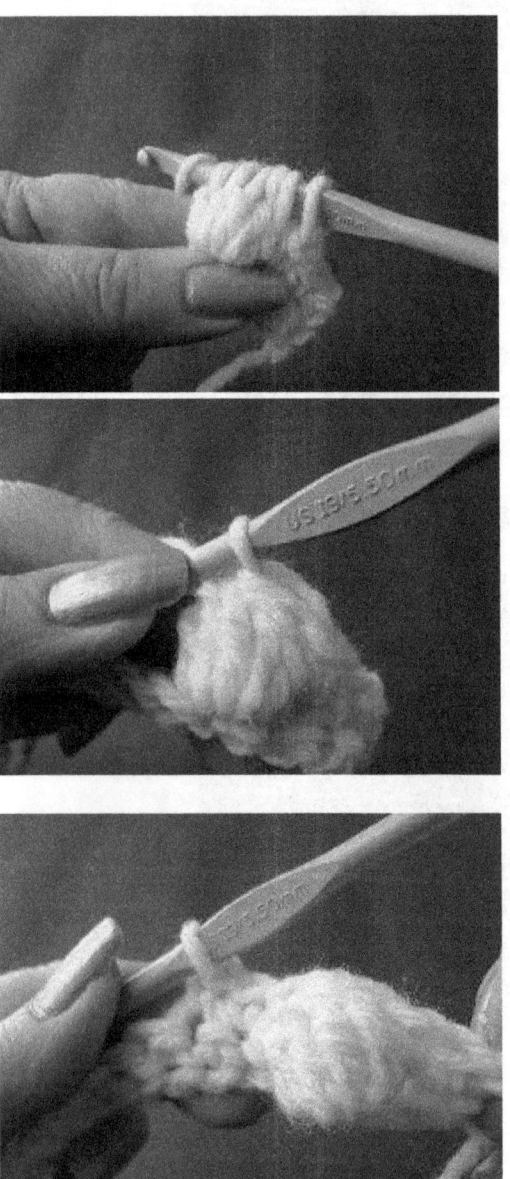

4. Repeat all of the given steps, and then chain 1 and turn your work again. Single crochet across the row once more.

5. Once again, repeat what you have done until you reach your desired shape and size of your project.

These are only basic crochet stitches to get you started. There are more complicated stitches that you can try, and they usually involve the basic stitches. If you already mastered the basic stitches, then learning the other stitches should not be that hard. Now it's time to try your newly acquired skill.

CHAPTER 4

Simple Patterns to Try

It's time to see if you can read the pattern and follow correctly. These are just simple patterns to motivate you further.

Cute White Flower

Do ch 5 and join both ends with sl st to form a ring.

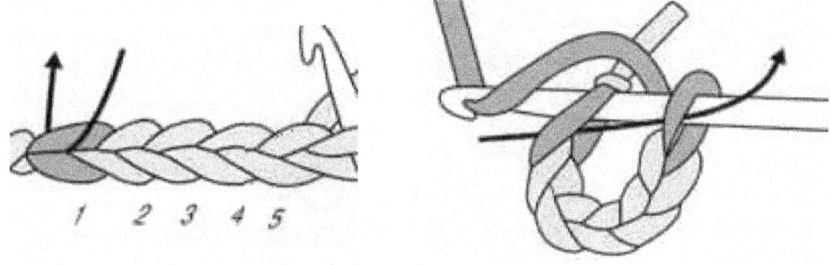

Rnd 1: Ch 1, sc 12 around the ring. Sl st to close.

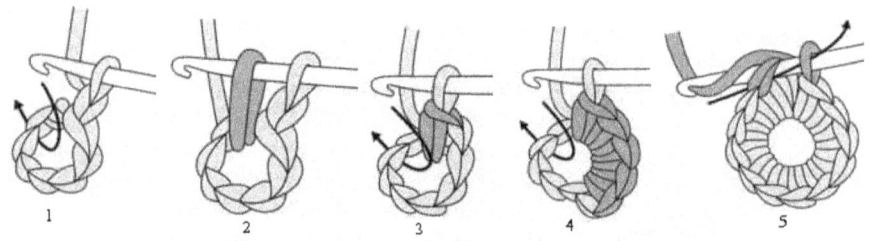

Rnd 2: 2 sc on each sc, around. Sl st to join. You will have 24 scs on your second row.

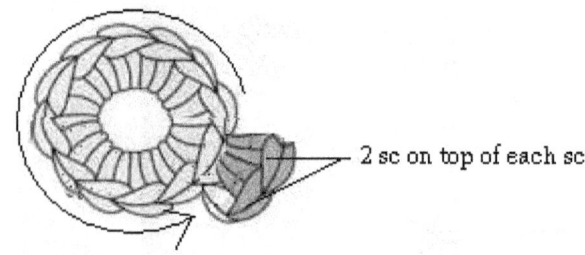

2 sc on top of each sc

Rnd 3: [ch 3, sk next sc, dc each in the next 2 sc, sk, ch 3, sl st on the next sc] around. On the last ch 3, sl st on the second chain of the first ch 3. Fasten off.

Golden Daisy

Do ch 6 and join both ends with sl st to form a ring.

Dc 12 around the ring. Sl st to close.

[Ch 5 plus ch 3 (t-ch), dc 3 on the next ch stitches (t-ch included), hdc 2 on the next 2 ch stitches, sc 1 on the next ch, sl st on top of next dc] around. Fasten off.

This is just the start. Keep practicing and try making your own design. Start with simple designs and don't stop having fun.

Baby Square

This is a doily that you could display in your living room or bedroom. It will definitely give your home that classic and cool appeal!

You will need:

4-ply medium/ bulky yarn in white (A), pink(B), and petal pink (C)

Hook size: 8 to 5.0 mm

Square size: 7 x 7"

Instructions:

Round 1: Use Color A. Ch 3, make 11 DCs in ring; use sl st to join until the top of beg ch 3, and end with sl st.

Round 2: Ch 3, and DC in the same spot. Make 2 DCs in next 2 sts, and then ch 3. Repeat thrice. Make sure to do 2 DCs in the next 3 sts, and then chain 3. End with sl st at beg-3 ch. This will make 24 DCs, and 4 ch-sps.

Round 3: Ch 3 and then make DCs in next st, ch 2, sk 2 sts, DC next 2 sts. This means you have to DC, ch 3, and then DC once again. Next DC in next 2 sts, ch 2, sk 2 sts, dc next 2 sts. Again, this means DC, ch 3, and DC until you reach the corner. Repeat twice and end with sl st on beg ch 3. Finish with 24 DC, 4 ch, 3 sps, ch 2 sps.

Round 4: Now, use Color B. Start by using sl st in the corner to join, and then ch 3, 2 dc, ch 3, 3 dc in the said corner. *Next, dc in next 3 sts, work in front of ch 2, sp tr in next 2 sk sts, dc next 3 sts)* This means 3 dc, ch 2, 3 dc in corner, and then repeat * to *. Do this twice, and use another sl st to join to the top of beg ch 3.

Round 5: Start with sl st to the corner, ch 3, 2 dc in cluster mode. *Next, sk 2 sts, sl st in next st or ch sp, ch 3, 2 dc in same st or sp, again in cluster mode* Repeat * to * twice and sl st to 3rd ch of beg ch 6. Finish with 24 dc, ch 3-sps.

Round 6: Ch 6 and dc in same st. *ch 3, sk cluster, dc next sl st, repeat 4 times, ch 3* This means dc, ch 3, dc in the corner, and end with sl st. Repeat * to * twice, and join using sl st from beg ch 6. Finish with 24 dc, 24 ch 3 sps.

Round 7: Now, use color C so you could join the corner with sl st, and then ch 3. This means 2 dc, ch3, 3dc in the said corner. *Now, dc next ch 3 sp, LDC between sts 1 and 2 of 2nd cluster row, dc current ch 3 sp, and repeat until the corner* 3 dc, ch 3, 3 dc, and then repeat * to * twice and end with sl st. Finish with 64 dc, 24 LDC, 4 ch 3 sps.

Shells and More Shells Scarf

Perfect for the fall and winter seasons, this project is meant to keep you warm—and fashionable, all the same!

You will need:

Light/mohair yarn

Hook size: 9.0 mm

Size: 7.5" x 58"

Instructions:

Start with base ch 26.

Row 1: From 2nd ch from hook, make sc. *skip 2 ch, 5 dc next ch, sk 2 ch, sc next ch* Repeat * to * until you see 3 remaining chains. Sk next 2 sts, sc last ch.

Row 2: Ch 3, turn, 2 dc 1st sc, *skip 2 sts, sc next dc, 5 dc next sc* Repeat * to * twice and then skip next 2 sts, sc next dc, 3 dc last stitch. You'd now have 3 whole shells and 2 half shells.

Row 3: Ch 1, turn, sc 1st st, *5 dc next sc, sk next 2 sts, sc next st* Repeat * to * across, and end with sc on top of 4th chain

Rows 4 to 30: Alternately repeat rows 2 to 3 until row 30, or just until your project measures 27", and then end with a 2nd completed row. Make sure not to fasten off.

For the edging:

Row 31: Ch 3, and turn, then sk 1st dc, sc in each of your next 3 sts, *ch 3, sk next 3 sts, dc next 3 sts*, Repeat * to * across, and end with ch 3, sc last st.

Row 32: Turn your work, sl st into 1st ch 3 arch, ch 4 same side. This means dc, ch 1, dc. *Skip next sc, sc next dc, next ch 3 arch, work dc, ch1, dc, ch1, dc, ch1, dc* Repeat * to * twice. In the final arch, do: dc, ch1, dc, ch1, dc.

Row 33: Ch 1, turn, sc each stitch until the end of your chain stitch. Make sure to fasten off. Weave ends to finish.

Chic Soap Pouch

This one is your simple air freshener—and a way of giving more life to your soap!

You will need:

100% plastic canvas/ nylon yarn

soap

Hook size: 8.0 mm

Instructions:

To start, make 12 chains. This will be the base of your soap pouch.

Round 1: From the 2nd chain on the hook, make sc. Ch 3, skip next ch, ch next ch 5 times, ch 3, sc in same st, ch 3, skip next st, sc next ch 5 times, ch 1. Then, join stitches together with hdc and then proceed to make sc so you'd be able to form the final loop. 3 loops = 12 chains.

Round 2: Ch 3, sc next ch 3 loop 11 times, ch 1. Join with hdc in first sc in order to form the last loop. Remember 3 loops = 12 chains.

Rounds 3 to 15: Repeat what you did in the 2nd round and then fasten off.

To make the drawstring, chain 150, and fasten off after.

To finish drawstring, make sure that you weave through at least 13 loops, and then tie the ends of the said drawstring together. You may also try letting ends pass through a flaming candle just to secure the ends. Insert the soap inside, close the drawstring, and hang in your bathroom—or any other place in the house!

Conclusion

Crocheting is a worthwhile hobby. Studies showed that the repetitive action in crocheting is a good stress buster. It can help calm the mind and body. It may be an age old craft, but it never goes out of style. It is fun to do and won't eat too much of your time or money.

Thank you again for downloading this book!

I hope this book was able to help you learn the craft called crocheting.

The next step is to keep enhancing your skill and share it with friends and family.

Finally, if you enjoyed this book, please take the time to share your thoughts and post a positive review on Amazon. It'd be greatly appreciated!

Thank you and good luck!